Okay-okay! I know you're eager to start training

HOW TO USE THIS bʋʋʀ

This book is divided into three distinct parts:

1. Hiragana and katakana writing practice sheets

The fact of the matter is that you'll probably have to use up a lot of practice paper before you memorize Japanese hiragana and katakana symbols. Of course nothing will make us happier than if you bought a new workbook everytime you use up an old one but if you're mindful of your budget here's what you can do. This workbook is designed in a way that you can cut out pages out of it or just stick them into a copying machine and copy them as much as you like for unlimited writing practice!

2. JLPT Level N5 vocabulary

Chances are that your first measurable goal in Japanese language learning is going to be to pass the Japanese Language Proficiency test Level N5. There's no official vocabulary for this test as of 2010 however there're estimates of what words are likely to show up based prior years' tests. In this book you will find such a vocabulary. There's no better way to learn words than to write them down, so here you have something to practice your newly obtained knowledge of hiragana and katakana symbols!

3. Cut out hiragana and katakana flash cards

Flash cards are a great way to learn however they are somewhat of a bummer to make by yourself and can be quite costly to buy. For that reason the on the last pages of this workbook we have placed hiragana and katakana flash cards that you can cut out yourself. Of course these would not be as cool as the cardboard ones however we've felt that it will be a nice extra thing to have. On the cards you will find some of the words from JLPT Level N5 vocabulary to memorize along with the symbols.

So, let me not hold you any further!

(Benkyō shiyou! - Let's study!)

Lilas Lingvo

Contents

Check out our 3-in-1 Kanji Workbook!

If you study Japanese you will have to learn not only kana characters but also a lot of kanji symbols.
To help you learn we have developed a special workbook that contains kanji writing practice sheets for 103 symbols needed for JLPT Level N5 with stroke order as well as cut-out flash cards for these symbols. Look it up on Amazon!
Below you can find a sample page from this book!

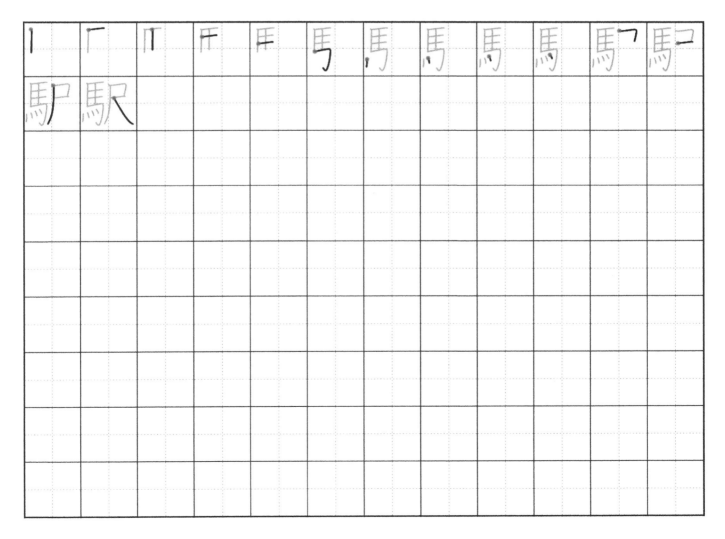

駅

station	
onyomi	エキ
kunyomi	の.む, -の.み
compounds	駅 えき station (n)
	駅員 えきいん station attendant (n)
	駅前 えきまえ in front of station (n)

Hiragana letters chart

gojūon

	a-column	*i*-column	*u*-column	*e*-column	*o*-column
a-row	あ a	い i	う u	え e	お o
ka-row	か ka	き ki	く ku	け ke	こ ko
sa-row	さ sa	し shi	す su	せ se	そ so
ta-row	た ta	ち chi	つ tsu	て te	と to
na-row	な na	に ni	ぬ nu	ね ne	の no
ha-row	は ha	ひ hi	ふ fu	へ he	ほ ho
ma-row	ま ma	み mi	む mu	め me	も mo
ya-row	や ya	い i	ゆ yu	え e	よ yo
ra-row	ら ra	り ri	る ru	れ re	ろ ro
wa-row	わ wa	い i	う u	え e	を o
	ん n				

yōon

きゃ kya	きゅ kyu	きょ kyo
しゃ sha	しゅ shu	しょ sho
ちゃ cha	ちゅ chu	ちょ cho
にゃ nya	にゅ nyu	にょ nyo
ひゃ hya	ひゅ hyu	ひょ hyo
みゃ mya	みゅ myu	みょ myo
りゃ rya	りゅ ryu	りょ ryo

dakuon

ga-row	が ga	ぎ gi	ぐ gu	げ ge	ご go
za-row	ざ za	じ ji	ず zu	ぜ ze	ぞ zo
da-row	だ da	ぢ ji	づ zu	で de	ど do
ba-row	ば ba	び bi	ぶ bu	べ be	ぼ bo

ぎゃ gya	ぎゅ gyu	ぎょ gyo
じゃ ja	じゅ ju	じょ jo
ぢゃ ja	ぢゅ ju	ぢょ jo
びゃ bya	びゅ byu	びょ byo

han-dakuon

pa-row	ぱ pa	ぴ pi	ぷ pu	ぺ pe	ぽ po

ぴゃ pya	ぴゅ pyu	ぴょ pyo

additional letters for foreign sounds

ゔ	ぁ	ぃ	ぅ	ぇ	ぉ

e.g. ゔぃ (vi), ふぁ (fa), てぃ (ti), どぅ (du), うぇ (we), ふぉ (fo)

sokuon

つ
pause (no sound)

Katakana letters chart

gojūon

	a-column	*i*-column	*u*-column	*e*-column	*o*-column
a-row	ア a	イ i	ウ u	エ e	オ o
ka-row	カ ka	キ ki	ク ku	ケ ke	コ ko
sa-row	サ sa	シ shi	ス su	セ se	ソ so
ta-row	タ ta	チ chi	ツ tsu	テ te	ト to
na-row	ナ na	ニ ni	ヌ nu	ネ ne	ノ no
ha-row	ハ ha	ヒ hi	フ fu	ヘ he	ホ ho
ma-row	マ ma	ミ mi	ム mu	メ me	モ mo
ya-row	ヤ ya	イ i	ユ yu	エ e	ヨ yo
ra-row	ラ ra	リ ri	ル ru	レ re	ロ ro
wa-row	ワ wa	イ i	ウ u	エ e	ヲ o

ン n

dakuon

	a-column	*i*-column	*u*-column	*e*-column	*o*-column
ga-row	ガ ga	ギ gi	グ gu	ゲ ge	ゴ go
za-row	ザ za	ジ ji	ズ zu	ゼ ze	ゾ zo
da-row	ダ da	ヂ ji	ヅ zu	デ de	ド do
ba-row	バ ba	ビ bi	ブ bu	ベ be	ボ bo

han-dakuon

pa-row	パ pa	ピ pi	プ pu	ペ pe	ポ po

additional letters for foreign sounds

ヴ ァ ィ ゥ ェ ォ

e.g. ヴィ (vi), ファ (fa), ティ (ti), ドゥ (du), ウェ (we), フォ (fo)

yōon

キャ kya	キュ kyu	キョ kyo
シャ sha	シュ shu	ショ sho
チャ cha	チュ chu	チョ cho
ニャ nya	ニュ nyu	ニョ nyo
ヒャ hya	ヒュ hyu	ヒョ hyo
ミャ mya	ミュ myu	ミョ myo
リャ rya	リュ ryu	リョ ryo
ギャ gya	ギュ gyu	ギョ gyo
ジャ ja	ジュ ju	ジョ jo
ヂャ ja	ヂュ ju	ヂョ jo
ビャ bya	ビュ byu	ビョ byo
ピャ pya	ピュ pyu	ピョ pyo

sokuon

ツ

pause (no sound)

あ	¹＝	²十	³あ	あ							**あ**
あ											a
あ											
あ											
あ											
あ											
あ											
あ											
あ											
あ											
あ											
あ											
あ											
あ											
あ											
あ											

a

Hiragana practice

い い | ¹い | い ²い | い い

い い

い い

い い

い い

い い

い い

い い

い い

い い

い い

い い

い い

い

う

| え | | え | え | | | | | | | | え |
| | | | | | | | | | | | e |

え
え
え
え
え
え
え
え
え
え
え
え
え
え
え

お

お | 1 → | 2 お | 3 お | お

お
o

お
お
お
お
お
お
お
お
お
お
お
お
お
お

か　か　か　か　か　　　　　　　　　　　　か
　　　　　　　　　　　　　　　　　　　　　ka

か

か

か

か

か

か

か

か

か

か

か

か

か

か

き

き

ki

き
き
き
き
き
き
き
き
き
き
き
き
き
き
き

く

ku

け け ¹け ²け ³け け

け

け

け

け

け

け

け

け

け

け

け

け

け

け

け

け

こ

ko

こ

Ah! Oh!

| あ | あ | | | | | | | | | | | |

to meet, to see

| あ | う | | | | | | | | | | | |

blue

| あ | お | い | | | | | | | | | | |

red

| あ | か | い | | | | | | | | | | |

autumn, fall

| あ | き | | | | | | | | | | | |

to open

| あ | く | | | | | | | | | | | |

no

| い | い | え | | | | | | | | | | |

to say

| い | う | | | | | | | | | | | |

how, in what way

| い | か | が | | | | | | | | | | |

to go

| い | く | | | | | | | | | | | |

pond

いけ

above, on top of

うえ

movie, film

えいが

English language

えいご

many

おおい

big

おおきい

to put, to place

おく

foreign country

がいこく

to buy

かう

face (person)

かお

keys

かぎ

to write

かく

tree, wood

き

to listen, to hear

きく

voice

こえ

here, this place

here, this place

ここ

medical science

いがく

to visit, to ask

うかがう

to move

うごく

hundred million

おく

meeting, conference

かいぎ

science

かがく

chance, opportunity

きかい

condition, state, health

ぐあい

air, atmosphere

くうき

airport

くうこう

plan, project, schedule

けいかく

experience

けいけん

suburb

こうがい

lecture

こうぎ

さ

さ

し　　　し　　　し　　　　　　　　　　　　　　　　　　　　　　し
shi

し

し

し

し

し

し

し

し

し

し

し

し

し

す	1 →	2 す	す								**す** su
す											
す											
す											
す											
す											
す											
す											
す											
す											
す											
す											
す											
す											
す											
す											

せ	→	#	せ	せ								せ
せ												se
せ												
せ												
せ												
せ												
せ												
せ												
せ												
せ												
せ												
せ												
せ												
せ												
せ												
せ												
せ												

そ	そ	そ									そ
そ											so
そ											
そ											
そ											
そ											
そ											
そ											
そ											
そ											
そ											
そ											
そ											
そ											
そ											

た	¹→ た	²た	³た	⁴た	た						た
た											ta
た											
た											
た											
た											
た											
た											
た											
た											
た											
た											
た											
た											
た											

ち	⇒	ち	ち								ち
ち											chi
ち											
ち											
ち											
ち											
ち											
ち											
ち											
ち											
ち											
ち											
ち											
ち											
ち											
ち											

つ

¹つ つ

つ

tsu

て | て | て
て
て
て
て
て
て
て
て
て
て
て
て
て

て

と

と

と

と

と

と

と

と

と

と

と

と

と

と

と

と

the future, former, previous

さき

to bloom

さく

salt

しお

however, but

しかし

work, employment

しごと

quite, peaceful

しずか

under, below

した

seven

しち

to smoke, to breathe in

すう

liking, fondness, love

すき

immediately, instantly

すぐ

little, few

すこし

cool, refreshing

すずしい

pupil

せいと

height, stature

せい

appears, to be the case

そうです

cleaning, sweeping

そうじ

and, like that

そうして

that place, there

そこ

outside, exterior

そと

counter for vehicles and machines

だい

university

だいがく

very likeable, like very

だいすき

important

たいせつ

tall, high, expensive

たかい

to put out, to send

だす

to stand

たつ

length, height

たて

small, little

ちいさい

near, close by, short

ちかい

to differ (from)

ち | が | う

underground train, subway

ち | か | て | つ

map

ち | ず

to use

つ | か | う

next

つ | ぎ

desk

つ | く | え

to arrive, to reach

つ | く

exit

で | ぐ | ち

why? for what reason?

ど | う | し | て

far, distant

と | お | い

な	1 →	2	3	4 な	な						な
な											na
な											
な											
な											
な											
な											
な											
な											
な											
な											
な											
な											
な											
な											

に	に	に	に	に	に							に
に	に	に	に	に	に							ni
に											
に											
に											
に											
に											
に											
に											
に											
に											
に											
に											
に											
に											
に											

ぬ	ぬ	ぬ	ぬ	ぬ	ぬ	ぬ	ぬ	ぬ	**ぬ**
ぬ	ぬ	ぬ	ぬ	ぬ	ぬ	ぬ	ぬ	ぬ	nu
ぬ									
ぬ									
ぬ									
ぬ									
ぬ									
ぬ									
ぬ									
ぬ									
ぬ									
ぬ									
ぬ									
ぬ									
ぬ									
ぬ									

ね	ね¹	²ね	ね	ね	ね	ね	ね	ね				**ね** ne
ね	ね	ね	ね	ね	ね	ね						
ね												
ね												
ね												
ね												
ね												
ね												
ね												
ね												
ね												
ね												
ね												
ね												
ね												

の　の　の　の　の　の　の　の　　　　　　　の
no

は は¹ は² は は は は

は は は は は は

は
は
は
は
は
は
は
は
は
は
は
は
は
は

は

ha

ひ ひ ひ ひ ひ ひ ひ ひ ひ ひ

ひ ひ ひ ひ ひ ひ ひ ひ ひ ひ

ひ

hi

ひ

ひ

ひ

ひ

ひ

ひ

ひ

ひ

ひ

ひ

ひ

ひ

ひ

ふ

fu

へ	1へ	へ	へ	へ	へ	へ	へ	へ	へ	へ
へ										he
へ										
へ										
へ										
へ										
へ										
へ										
へ										
へ										
へ										
へ										
へ										
へ										
へ										

Hiragana practice

ほ	ほ	に	に	ほ	ほ	ほ	ほ	ほ	ほ	ほ

ほ
ho

ほ										
ほ										
ほ										
ほ										
ほ										
ほ										
ほ										
ほ										
ほ										
ほ										
ほ										
ほ										
ほ										
ほ										
ほ										

inside, middle, among

なか

long

ながい

to sing (bird), to make sound (animal)

なく

to lose something

なくす

meat

にく

west

にし

to take off clothes

ぬぐ

cat

ねこ

yes

はい

postcard

はがき

to wear, to put on

| は | く | | | | | | | | | | |

box

| は | こ | | | | | | | | | | |

bridge, chopsticks

| は | し | | | | | | | | | | |

beginning, start

| は | じ | め | | | | | | | | | |

for the first time

| は | じ | め | て | | | | | | | | |

20 years, 20 years old

| は | た | ち | | | | | | | | | |

flower

| は | な | | | | | | | | | | |

talk, story

| は | な | し | | | | | | | | | |

to speak

| は | な | す | | | | | | | | | |

to pull, to play piano

| ひ | く | | | | | | | | | | |

short, low

| び | く | い | | | | | | | | | | | |

airplane

| ひ | こ | う | き | | | | | | | | | |

man, person

| ひ | と | | | | | | | | | | | |

one month

| ひ | と | つ | き | | | | | | | | | |

to blow (wind), clothes

| ふ | く | | | | | | | | | | | |

two

| ふ | た | つ | | | | | | | | | | |

pork

| ぶ | た | に | く | | | | | | | | | |

second day of the month

| ふ | つ | か | | | | | | | | | | |

fat, thick

| ふ | と | い | | | | | | | | | | |

unskillful, poor

| へ | た | | | | | | | | | | | |

way

ほう

hat

ぼうし

other place, the rest

ほか

want, in need of, desire

ほしい

to cry, to weep

なく

fever, temperature

ねつ

throat

のど

to transport, to carry

はこぶ

drawer

ひきだし

compexity, complication

ふくざつ

ま | 1→ 2→ | ニ→ | ま | ま | | | | | | | **ま**
ma

ま
ま
ま
ま
ま
ま
ま
ま
ま
ま
ま
ま
ま
ま

み	み	み	み	み	み	み	み	み	み	**み**
										mi
み										
み										
み										
み										
み										
み										
み										
み										
み										
み										
み										
み										
み										
み										
み										

む

| む | む | む | む | む | む | む | む | む | **む**
mu |

| め | め | め | め | め | め | め | め | め | め | **め** |
| | | | | | | | | | | me |

め
め
め
め
め
め
め
め
め
め
め
め
め
め

も　し　も　も　も　も　も　も　も　も

も
mo

や	¹う	²う	³や	や	や						や
や											ya
や											
や											
や											
や											
や											
や											
や											
や											
や											
や											
や											
や											
や											

ゆ	ゆ	ゆ	ゆ	ゆ	ゆ	ゆ	ゆ	ゆ	ゆ	ゆ
ゆ										**ゆ**
ゆ										yu
ゆ										
ゆ										
ゆ										
ゆ										
ゆ										
ゆ										
ゆ										
ゆ										
ゆ										
ゆ										
ゆ										
ゆ										

よ

よ   ¹⇌ ²よ よ よ よ よ よ   よ
                                                          yo

よ

よ

よ

よ

よ

よ

よ

よ

よ

よ

よ

よ

よ

よ

よ

every morning

ま	い	あ	さ								

everyday

ま	い	に	ち								

before, in front

ま	え										

unappetising, unpleasant

ま	ず	い									

again, and

ま	た										

town, city

ま	ち										

to wait

ま	つ										

window

ま	ど										

to brush (teeth)

み	が	く									

right-hand side

み	ぎ										

short

みじかい

water

みず

store, shop, establishment

みせ

road, street

みち

everyone

みなさん

south

みなみ

six days, sixth (day of

むいか

beyond, over there

むこう

village

むら

spectacles, eye glasses

めがね

already

もう

hello (on the phone)

もしもし

to hold, to carry, to possess

もつ

thing, object

もの

greengrocer

やおや

vegetable

やさい

easy, plain, simple

やさしい

cheap, inexpensive

やすい

rest, vacation

やすみ

evening

ゆうがた

famous

ゆうめい

snow

ゆき

eight days, the eighth (day of the month)

ようか

Western-style clothes

ようふく

often

よく

to call out, to invite

よぶ

to read

よむ

last night

ゆうべ

soon, very soon

もうすぐ

dream

ゆめ

| ら | ¹ら | ²ら | ら | ら | ら | ら | ら | ら | ら | **ら** |
| | | | | | | | | | | ra |

ら

ら

ら

ら

ら

ら

ら

ら

ら

ら

ら

ら

ら

ら

| り | り¹ | り² | り | り | り | り | り | り | り | り |
| り | | | | | | | | | | ri |
| り |
| り |
| り |
| り |
| り |
| り |
| り |
| り |
| り |
| り |
| り |
| り |
| り |
| り |

る	る	る	る	る	る	る	る	る	る	**る**
										ru
る										
る										
る										
る										
る										
る										
る										
る										
る										
る										
る										
る										
る										
る										

れ　れ　れ　れ　れ　れ　れ　れ　れ

れ

re

ろ　ろ　ろ　ろ　ろ　ろ　ろ　ろ　ろ　ろ　　ろ
ro

ろ
ろ
ろ
ろ
ろ
ろ
ろ
ろ
ろ
ろ
ろ
ろ
ろ
ろ

| わ | ①↓ | ②わ | わ | わ | わ | わ | わ | わ | **わ** |
| --- | --- | --- | --- | --- | --- | --- | --- | --- | wa |

わ
わ
わ
わ
わ
わ
わ
わ
わ
わ
わ
わ
わ
わ

を	を	を	を	を	を						を
を											
を											
を											
を											
を											
を											
を											
を											
を											
を											
を											
を											
を											

o

65

ん	ん	ん									ん
											n/m
ん											
ん											
ん											
ん											
ん											
ん											
ん											
ん											
ん											
ん											
ん											
ん											

next month

らいげつ

cooking, cuisine

りょうり

zero, nought

れい

corridor

ろうか

young

わかい

to understand

わかる

to forget

わすれる

bad, inferior

わるい

to cross over, to go across

わたる

cooling, air conditioning

れいぼう

history

れ き し

communication, contact, connection

れ ん ら く

to boil

わ く

to laugh, to smile

わ ら う

to break

わ れ る

Japanese hotel, inn

り ょ か ん

parents, both parents

り ょ う し ん

six

ろ く

I, myself

わ た し

next year

ら い ね ん

ア ア ア ア ア ア

ア

a

イ イ イ イ イ イ

イ
i

ウ	ウ	ウ	ヲ	ウ	ウ	ウ					ウ
ウ											u

ウ

ウ

ウ

ウ

ウ

ウ

ウ

ウ

ウ

ウ

ウ

ウ

ウ

ウ

エ	1 →	2	3 →								エ
											e
エ											
エ											
エ											
エ											
エ											
エ											
エ											
エ											
エ											
エ											
エ											
エ											
エ											

オ オ⃗ オ↓ オ オ オ オ

オ

力　カ　カ　カ　カ　カ

力

力

力

力

力

力

力

力

力

力

力

力

力

力

力
ka

キ

ク ク ⃗ク ク ク ク

ク
ku

ク
ク
ク
ク
ク
ク
ク
ク
ク
ク
ク
ク
ク
ク

ケ

ケ

ke

コ ユ

コ
ko

サ	¹サ	²サ	³サ	サ	サ	サ						サ
												sa

サ

サ

サ

サ

サ

サ

サ

サ

サ

サ

サ

サ

サ

サ

シ

shi

ス	ス	ス	ス	ス	ス					ス
ス										su

セ　セ　セ　セ　セ　セ

セ

セ

セ

セ

セ

セ

セ

セ

セ

セ

セ

セ

セ

セ

| ソ | ソ | ソ | | | | | | | | | ソ |
| | | | | | | | | | | | so |

												タ
タ	ᵗ⁄⁄	²フ	³彡	タ	タ	タ						ta
タ												
タ												
タ												
タ												
タ												
タ												
タ												
タ												
タ												
タ												
タ												
タ												
タ												
タ												

チ	チ	チ	リ	チ	チ	チ					チ
チ											chi
チ											
チ											
チ											
チ											
チ											
チ											
チ											
チ											
チ											
チ											
チ											
チ											
チ											

ツ ツ ツ¹ ツ² ツ³ ツ ツ ツ

ツ
tsu

テ	テ	テ	テ	テ	テ	テ					テ
テ											te
テ											
テ											
テ											
テ											
テ											
テ											
テ											
テ											
テ											
テ											
テ											
テ											

ト　↓　↗　ト　ト　ト　　　　　　　　　ト
　　　　　　　　　　　　　　　　　　　to

ナ	ナ	ナ²	ナ	ナ	ナ						ナ
											na

	1 →											ニ
		2 →										ni

ヌ ヲ ヌ ヌ ヌ ヌ

ヌ
nu

ヌ
ヌ
ヌ
ヌ
ヌ
ヌ
ヌ
ヌ
ヌ
ヌ
ヌ
ヌ
ヌ
ヌ

ネ ネ ネ ネ ネ ネ ネ ネ

ネ
ne

ノ

no

Katakana practice

八 八 八 八 八 八 八 八

八

ha

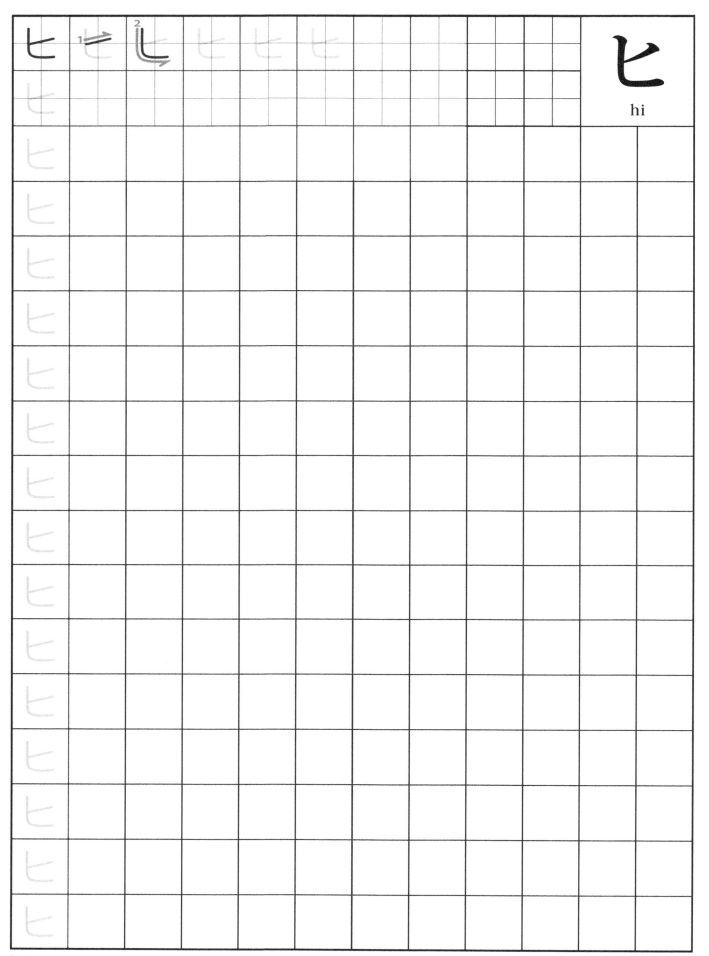

ヒ

hi

フ フ フ フ フ

フ

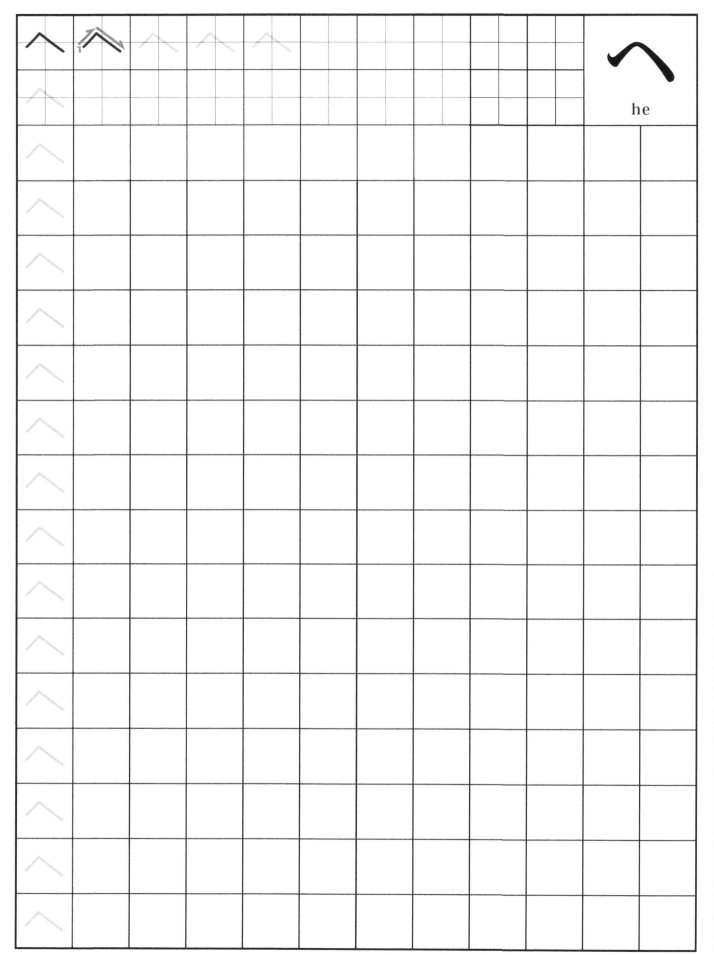

he

ホ	→	↓²	³ホ	ホ⁴	ホ	ホ	ホ					ホ
												ho

ホ
ホ
ホ
ホ
ホ
ホ
ホ
ホ
ホ
ホ
ホ
ホ
ホ
ホ
ホ

マ　マ　マ　マ　マ　マ

マ

ma

マ
マ
マ
マ
マ
マ
マ
マ
マ
マ
マ
マ
マ

	1 →	2 →	3 →								ミ
											mi

ム ム ム ム ム ム

ム
mu

メ

me

モ	モ	モ	モ	モ	モ	モ				モ
モ										
モ										
モ										
モ										
モ										
モ										
モ										
モ										
モ										
モ										
モ										
モ										
モ										
モ										
モ										

mo

ヤ ヤ ヤ ヤ ヤ ヤ

ヤ

ユ ユ ユ ユ ユ ユ ユ ユ

ユ

yu

ヨ ヨ ヨ ヨ ヨ ヨ ヨ

ヨ

yo

ラ ラ ラ ラ ラ ラ

ラ
ra

リ　リ　リ　リ　リ　リ

リ

 リ

ル　ル　ル　ル　ル　ル　　　　　　　ル
ru

レ

re

ロ

1
2
3

ロ

ワ ワ ワ ワ ワ ワ

ワ

wa

ヲ ヲ ヲ ノ ヲ ヲ ヲ ヲ

apartment

ア	パ	ー	ト								

elevator

エ	レ	ベ	ー	タ	ー						

cup

カ	ッ	プ									

camera

カ	メ	ラ									

curry

カ	レ	ー									

calendar

カ	レ	ン	ダ	ー							

guitar

ギ	タ	ー									

kilo (kilogram, kilometer)

キ	ロ										

gram

グ	ラ	ム									

meter

メ	ー	ト	ル								

class

クラス

coat

コート

coffee

コーヒー

copy

コピ

shirt

シャツ

shower

シャワー

skirt

スカート

heater, stove

ストーブ

spoon

スプーン

sport

スポーツ

trousers

ズボン

slippers

スリッパ

zero

ゼロ

taxi

タクシー

tape

テープ

recorder

レコーダー

table

テーブル

test

テスト

department store

デパート

television

テレビ

door (Western style)

ド | ア

toilet

ト | イ | レ

knife

ナ | イ | フ

news

ニ | ュ | ー | ス

tie, necktie

ネ | ク | タ | イ

party

パ | ー | テ | ィ | ー

bus

バ | ス

butter

バ | タ | ー

bread

パ | ン

handkerchief

ハ | ン | カ | チ

film (roll of)

フィルム

swimming pool

プール

fork

フォーク

bed

ベッド

pet

ペット

pen

ペン

ball

ボール

pocket

ポケット

post

ポスト

button

ボタン

hotel

ホテル

match

マッチ

radio

ラジオ

radio cassette player

ラジカセ

restaurant

レストラン

business shirt

ワイシャツ

bell

ベル

present, gift

プレゼント

building (abbreviation), bill

ビル

piano

ピアノ

#	Kana	Kanji	Type	Definition
1	あう	会う	u-v	to meet, to see
2	あお	青	n	blue
3	あおい	青い	adj	blue
4	あか	赤	n	red
5	あかい	赤い	adj	red
6	あかるい	明るい	adj	bright, cheerful
7	あき	秋	n-adv	autumn, fall
8	あく	開く	u-v,vi	to open, to become open
9	あける	開ける	ru-v	to open
10	あげる	上げる	ru-v	to give
11	あさ	朝	n-adv,n-t	morning
12	あさごはん	朝御飯	n	breakfast
13	あさって		n-adv,n-t	day after tomorrow
14	あし	足	n	foot, leg
15	あした		n-t	tomorrow
16	あそこ		n	there, over there, that place
17	あそぶ	遊ぶ	u-v	to play, to enjoy oneself
18	あたたかい	暖かい	adj	warm, mild
19	あたま	頭	n	head
20	あたらしい	新しい	adj	new
21	あちら		n	there, yonder, that
22	あつい	暑い	adj	hot, warm
23	あつい	熱い	adj	hot (thing)
24	あつい	厚い	adj	kind, warm(hearted), thick, deep
25	あっち		n col	over there

#	Kana	Kanji	Type	Definition
26	あと	後	adj-no,n	afterwards, since then, in the future
27	あなた		n	you
28	あに	兄	n	(hum) older brother
29	あね	姉	n	(hum) older sister
30	あの		pren-adj	that over there
31	あの		int	um...
32	アパート		n,adv	apartment (abbr)
33	あびる		ru-v	to bathe, to shower
34	あぶない	危ない	adj	dangerous, critical, watch out!
35	あまい	甘い	adj,expr	generous, sweet
36	あまり		na-adj,adv,n,n-suf	not very, not much
37	あめ	雨	n	rain
38	あめ	飴	n	(hard) candy, toffee
39	あらう	洗う	u-v	to wash
40	ある [存在]		u-v-i	to be
41	ある [所有]		u-v-i	to have
42	あるく	歩く	u-v	to walk
43	あれ		int,n	that, that thing
44	いい/よい		adj	good
45	いいえ		int,n	no, not at all
46	いう	言う	u-v	to say
47	いえ	家	n	house, family
48	いかが		na-adj,adv,n	how, in what way
49	いく/ゆく	行く	u-v	to go
50	いくつ		n	how many?, how old?

#	Kana	Kanji	Type	Definition
51	いくら		adv,n	how much?, how many?
52	いけ	池	n	pond
53	いしゃ	医者	n	doctor (medical)
54	いす		n	chair
55	いそがしい	忙しい	adj	busy, irritated
56	いたい	痛い	adj	painful
57	いち	一	num	one
58	いちにち	一日	n	1 day (duration)
59	いちばん		n-adv	best, first, number one
60	いつ		gn-adv	when
61	いつか	五日	n	five days, fifth day of the month
62	いっしょ	一緒	adv,n	together
63	いつつ	五つ	n	five
64	いつも		adv,n	always, every time
65	いぬ	犬	n	dog
66	いま	今		now
67	いみ	意味	n,vs	meaning
68	いもうと	妹	n	younger sister
69	いや	嫌	na-adj,n	disagreeable, no
70	いりぐち	入口	n	entrance, gate
71	いる	居る	u-v	(hum) to be (animate), to exist
72	いる	要る	u-v	to need
73	いれる	入れる	ru-v	to put in
74	いろ	色	n	colour
75	いろいろ		na-adj,adj-no,adv,n	various

#	Kana	Kanji	Type	Definition
76	うえ	上	no-adj,n-adv,n,n-suf	above, on top of
77	うしろ	後ろ	n	behind, rear
78	うすい	薄い	adj	thin, weak
79	うた	歌	n	song
80	うたう	歌う	u-v	to sing
81	うち		n	house (one's own)
82	うまれる	生まれる	ru-v	to be born
83	うみ	海	n	sea, beach
84	うる	売る	u-v	to sell
85	うるさい		adj	noisy, loud, annoying
86	うわぎ	上着	n	coat, jacket
87	え	絵	n,n-suf	picture, drawing, painting, sketch
88	えいが	映画	n	movie, film
89	えいがかん	映画館	n	movie theatre (theater), cinema
90	えいご	英語	n	the English language
91	ええ		conj,int,n	yes
92	えき	駅	n	station
93	エレベーター		n	elevator
94	〜えん	〜円	n	yen (currency)
95	えんぴつ	鉛筆	n	pencil
96	お〜		prefix	honourable 〜 (honorific)
97	おいしい		adj	delicious, tasty
98	おおい	多い	adj	many
99	おおきい	大きい	adj	big
100	おおきな	大きな	na-adj	big

#	Kana	Kanji	Type	Definition
101	おおぜい	大勢	n	great number of people
102	おかあさん	お母さん	n	(hon) mother
103	おかし	お菓子	n	confections, sweets, candy
104	おかね	お金	n	money
105	おきる	起きる	ru-v	to get up, to rise
106	おく	置く	u-v	to put, to place
107	おくさん	奥さん	n	(hon) wife
108	おさけ	お酒	n	alcohol, sake (rice wine)
109	おさら	お皿	n	plate, dish
110	おじ・さん	伯父/叔父・さん		uncle, middle aged man
111	おじいさん		n	grandfather, male senior citizen
112	おしえる	教える	ru-v	to teach, to inform
113	おす	押す	u-v,vt	to push, to press
114	おそい	遅い	adj	late, slow
115	おちゃ	お茶	n	tea (green)
116	おてあらい	お手洗い		toilet, lavatory, bathroom
117	おとうさん	お父さん	n	(hon) father
118	おとうと	弟	n	younger brother
119	おとこ	男	n	man
120	おとこのこ	男の子	n	boy
121	おととい		n-adv,n-t	day before yesterday
122	おととし		n-adv,n-t	year before last
123	おとな	大人	n	adult
124	おなか		n	stomach
125	おなじ	同じ	na-adj,n	same, identical, similar

#	Kana	Kanji	Type	Definition
126	おにいさん	お兄さん	n	(hon) older brother
127	おねえさん	お姉さん	n	(hon) older sister
128	おばさん	伯母さん/叔母さん		aunt
129	おばあさん		n	grandmother, female senior-citizen
130	おふろ	お風呂	n	bath
131	おべんとう	お弁当	n	boxed lunch
132	おぼえる	覚える	ru-v	to remember, to memorize
133	おまわりさん		n	policeman (friendly term)
134	おもい	重い	adj	heavy
135	おもしろい		adj	interesting, amusing
136	およぐ	泳ぐ	u-v	to swim
137	おりる	降りる	ru-v	to alight (eg from bus), to get off
138	おわる	終る	u-v	to finish, to close
139	おんがく	音楽	n	music
140	おんな	女	n	woman, girl, daughter
141	おんなのこ	女の子	n	girl
142	～かい	～回	n	counter for occurrences
143	～かい	～階	n	counter for storeys of a building
144	がいこく	外国	n	foreign country
145	がいこくじん	外国人	n	foreigner
146	かいしゃ	会社	n	company, corporation
147	かいだん	階段	n	stairs
148	かいもの	買い物	n	shopping
149	かう	買う	u-v	to buy
150	かえす	返す	u-v,vt	to return something

#	Kana	Kanji	Type	Definition
151	かえる	帰る	u-v	to go home, to return
152	かお	顔	n	face (person)
153	かかる		u-v,vi	to take (eg time, money)
154	かぎ		n	key/s
155	かく	書く	u-v	to write
156	がくせい	学生	n	student
157	〜かげつ	〜か月	suf	(number of) months
158	かける		ru-v	to put on (eg glasses)
159	かける		ru-v	to dial/call (eg phone)
160	かさ	傘	n	umbrella
161	かす	貸す	u-v	to lend
162	かぜ	風	n	wind, breeze
163	かぜ	風邪	n	cold, illness
164	かた	方	n	person
165	かぞく	家族	n	family
166	かたかな	片仮名	n	katakana
167	〜がつ	〜月	suf	month of year
168	がっこう	学校	n	school
169	カップ		n	cup
170	かてい	家庭	n	home, household
171	かど	角	n	corner (e.g. desk)
172	かばん		n	bag, basket
173	かびん	花瓶	n	(flower) vase
174	かぶる		u-v	to wear, to put on (head)
175	かみ	紙	n	paper

#	Kana	Kanji	Type	Definition
176	カメラ		n	camera
177	かようび	火曜日	n-adv,n	Tuesday
178	からい	辛い	adj	spicy, salty
179	からだ	体	n	body
180	かりる	借りる	ru-v	to borrow, to have a loan
181	～がる		suf	feel
182	かるい	軽い	adj	light, non-serious, minor
183	カレー		n	curry
184	カレンダー		n	calendar
185	かわ	川/河	n	river
186	～がわ	側	n-suf	～ side
187	かわいい		adj	cute, charming
188	かんじ	漢字	n	kanji, Chinese character
189	き	木	n	tree, wood
190	きいろ	黄色	n	yellow
191	きいろい	黄色い	adj	yellow
192	きえる	消える	ru-v	to go out, to vanish
193	きく	聞く	u-v	to hear, to listen, to ask
194	きた	北		north
195	ギター		n	guitar
196	きたない	汚い	adj	dirty, messy
197	きっさてん	喫茶店	n	coffee lounge
198	きって	切手	n	stamp (eg. postage)
199	きっぷ	切符	n	ticket
200	きのう	昨日	n-adv,n-t	yesterday

#	Kana	Kanji	Type	Definition
201	きゅう	九	num	nine
202	ぎゅうにく	牛肉	n	beef
203	ぎゅうにゅう	牛乳	n	milk
204	きょう	今日	n-t	today, this day
205	きょうしつ	教室	n	classroom
206	きょうだい	兄弟	n	siblings (brothers and sisters)
207	きょねん	去年	n-adv,n-t	last year
208	きらい	嫌い	na-adj,n	dislike, hate
209	きる	切る	suf,u-v	to cut, to chop
210	きる	着る	ru-v	to put on from shoulders down
211	きれい		na-adj	pretty, clean, nice, tidy
212	キロ/キログラム		n,pref	kilo (kilogram)
213	キロ/キロメートル		n,pref	kilo (kilometre)
214	ぎんこう	銀行	n	bank
215	きんようび	金曜日	n-adv,n	Friday
216	く	九	number	nine
217	くすり	薬	n	medicine
218	ください	kana only	(with te-form verb) please do for me
219	くだもの	果物	n	fruit
220	くち	口	n	mouth, orifice, opening
221	くつ	靴	n	shoes, footwear
222	くつした	靴下	n	socks
223	くに	国	n	country
224	くもり	曇り	adv	cloudiness, cloudy weather
225	くもる	曇る	u-v	to become cloudy, to become dim

#	Kana	Kanji	Type	Definition
226	くらい	暗い	adj	dark, gloomy
227	～くらい/ぐらい		suf	approximate (quantity)
228	クラス		n	class
229	グラム		n	gram
230	くる	来る	vk	to come
231	くるま	車	n	car, vehicle
232	くろ	黒	n	black
233	くろい	黒い	adj	black
234	けいかん	警官	n	policeman
235	けさ	今朝	n-temp	this morning
236	けす	消す	u-v	to erase, to delete, to turn off power
237	けっこう	結構	na-adj,n-adv,n	nice, enough
238	けっこん（する）	結婚	adj-no,n,vs	marriage
239	げつようび	月曜日	n-adv,n	Monday
240	げんかん	玄関	n	entrance-way, entry hall
241	げんき	元気	na-adj,n	health
242	～こ	～個	n,suf	counter for small items
243	ご	五	num	five
244	～ご	～語	n,n-suf	word, language
245	こうえん	公園	n	(public) park
246	こうさてん	交差点	n	intersection
247	こうちゃ	紅茶	n	black tea
248	こうばん	交番	n	police box
249	こえ	声	n	voice
250	コート		n	coat

#	Kana	Kanji	Type	Definition
251	コーヒー		n	coffee
252	ここ		n	here, this place
253	ごご	午後	n-adv,n-t	afternoon, P.M.
254	ここのか	九日		nine days, ninth day of the month
255	ここのつ	九つ	n	nine
256	ごぜん	午前	n-adv,n-t	morning, A.M.
257	こたえる	答える	ru-v	to answer, to reply
258	こちら		n	this eg person, way
259	こっち		n	this eg person, way
260	コップ		n	cup
261	ことし	今年	n-adv,n-t	this year
262	ことば	言葉	n	word
263	こども	子供	n	child, children
264	この		adj-pn,int	this
265	ごはん	御飯	n	rice (cooked), meal
266	コピー・する		n,p-suru	to copy
267	こまる	困る	u-v	to be worried, to be bothered
268	これ		int,n	this
269	〜ころ/〜ごろ		n-suf	about, approximately (time)
270	こんげつ	今月	n-adv,n-t	this month
271	こんしゅう	今週	n-adv,n-t	this week
272	こんな		na-adj,adj-pn,adv,n	such, like this
273	こんばん	今晩	n-adv,n-t	tonight, this evening
274	さあ		conj,int	come now, well
275	〜さい	〜歳	suf	〜years-old

#	Kana	Kanji	Type	Definition
276	さいふ	財布	n	wallet
277	さかな	魚	n	fish
278	さき	先		the future, former, previous
279	さく	咲く	u-v	to bloom
280	さくぶん	作文	n	composition, writing
281	さす	差す	u-v	to raise (stretch out) hands
282	〜さつ	〜冊	n	counter for books
283	ざっし	雑誌	n	magazine
284	さとう	砂糖	n	sugar
285	さむい	寒い	adj	cold (e.g. weather)
286	さらいねん	さ来年	n-adv,n-t	year after next
287	〜さん		suf	Mr or Mrs
288	さん	三	num	three
289	さんぽ（する）	散歩	n,vs	walk, stroll
290	し	四	num	four
291	〜じ	〜時	suf	time (〜 O'clock)
292	しお	塩	n	salt
293	しかし		conj	however, but
294	じかん	時間	n-adv,n	time
295	〜じかん	〜時間	suf	〜hours
296	しごと	仕事	adj-no,n	work, occupation, employment
297	じしょ	辞書	n	dictionary
298	しずか	静か	na-adj	quiet, peaceful
299	した	下	n	under, below, beneath
300	しち	七	num	seven

#	Kana	Kanji	Type	Definition
301	しつもん	質問	n,vs	question, inquiry
302	じてんしゃ	自転車	n	bicycle
303	じどうしゃ	自動車	n	automobile
304	しぬ	死ぬ	v5n	to die
305	じびき	字引	n	dictionary
306	じぶん	自分	n	myself, oneself
307	しまる	閉まる	u-v,vi	to close, to be closed
308	しめる	閉める	ru-v,vt	to close, to shut
309	しめる	締める	ru-v	to tie, to fasten
310	じゃ/じゃあ		conj,int	well, well then
311	しゃしん	写真	n	photograph
312	シャツ		n	shirt, singlet
313	シャワー		n	shower
314	じゅう	十	num	ten
315	〜じゅう	〜中	suf	during, while
316	〜しゅうかん	〜週間	suf	〜weeks
317	じゅぎょう	授業	n,vs	lesson, class work
318	しゅくだい	宿題	n	homework
319	じょうず	上手	na-adj,n	skill, skillful, dexterity
320	じょうぶ	丈夫	na-adj,n	strong, solid, durable
321	しょうゆ		n	soy sauce
322	しょくどう	食堂	n	cafeteria, dining hall
323	しる	知る	u-v	to know, to understand
324	しろ	白	n	white
325	しろい	白い	adj	white

#	Kana	Kanji	Type	Definition
326	〜にん	〜人	n,suf	counter for people
327	しんぶん	新聞	n	newspaper
328	すいようび	水曜日	n-adv,n	Wednesday
329	すう	吸う	u-v	to smoke, to breathe in, to suck
330	スカート		n	skirt
331	すき	好き	na-adj,n	liking, fondness, love
332	〜すぎ		suf	to exceed, 〜 too much
333	すくない	少ない	adj	a few, scarce
334	すぐ・に		adv	immediately, instantly
335	すこし	少し	adv,n	little, few
336	すずしい	涼しい	adj	cool, refreshing
337	〜ずつ		suf	at a time, gradually
338	ストーブ		n	heater (lit: stove)
339	スプーン		n	spoon
340	スポーツ		n	sport
341	ズボン		n	trousers (fr: jupon)
342	すむ	住む	u-v	to reside, to live in
343	スリッパ		n	slippers
344	する		vs-i	to do, to try
345	すわる	座る	u-v	to sit
346	せい	背	n	height, stature
347	せいと	生徒	n	pupil
348	セーター		n	sweater, jumper
349	せっけん	石鹸	n	soap
350	せびろ	背広	n	business suit

#	Kana	Kanji	Type	Definition
351	せまい	狭い	adj	narrow, confined, small
352	ゼロ		n	zero
353	せん	千		thousand, many
354	せんげつ	先月	n-adv,n-t	last month
355	せんしゅう	先週	n-adv,n-t	last week, the week before
356	せんせい	先生	n	teacher, master, doctor
357	せんたく	洗濯	n,vs	washing, laundry
358	ぜんぶ	全部	n-adv,n-t	all, entire, whole
359	そう/そうです			appears, to be the case
360	そうじ(する)	掃除	n,vs	cleaning, sweeping
361	そうして/そして		conj	and, like that
362	そこ		n	that place, there
363	そちら		n	over there
364	そっち		n	over there
365	そと	外	n	outside, exterior
366	その		adj-pn	that
367	そば		n	near, close, beside
368	そら	空	n	sky
369	それ		n	it, that
370	それから		uk	and then, after that
371	それでは		exp	in that situation, well then...
372	～だい	～台	suf	counter for vehicles/machines
373	だいがく	大学	n	university
374	たいしかん	大使館	n	embassy
375	だいじょうぶ	大丈夫	na-adj,adv,n	safe, all right, O.K.

#	Kana	Kanji	Type	Definition
376	だいすき	大好き	na-adj,n	very likeable, like very much
377	たいせつ	大切	na-adj,n	important
378	だいどころ	台所	n	kitchen
379	たいへん		na-adj,adv,n	very
380	たいへん		na-adj,adv,n	difficult situation, tough situation
381	たかい	高い	adj	tall, high
382	たかい	高い	adj	expensive
383	～だけ		prt	only ～, just ～
384	たくさん		na-adj,adv,n	many, a lot, much
385	タクシー		n	taxi
386	だす	出す	u-v	to put out, to send
387	～たち		n-suf	plural suffix
388	たつ	立つ	u-v	to stand
389	たて		n	length, height
390	たてもの	建物	n	building
391	たのしい	楽しい	adj	enjoyable, fun
392	たのむ	頼む	u-v	to request, to ask
393	たばこ		n	tobacco, cigarettes
394	たぶん		adv,n	perhaps, probably
395	たべもの	食べ物	n	food
396	たべる	食べる	ru-v	to eat
397	たまご	卵	n	egg(s)
398	だれ	誰	n	who
399	だれか	誰か	n	someone, somebody
400	たんじょうび	誕生日	n	birthday

#	Kana	Kanji	Type	Definition
401	だんだん		adv,n	gradually, by degrees
402	ちいさい	小さい	adj	small, little
403	ちいさな	小さな	na-adj	small, little
404	ちかい	近い	adj,suf	near, close by, short
405	ちがう	違う	u-v	to differ (from)
406	ちかく	近く	n-adv,n	near
407	ちかてつ	地下鉄	n	underground train, subway
408	ちず	地図	n	map
409	ちち	父	n	(one's own) father
410	ちゃいろ	茶色	n	brown
411	ちゃわん		n	rice bowl
412	〜ちゅう	〜中	suf	during, while 〜ing
413	ちょうど		gn	just, right, exactly
414	ちょっと		adv,int	a little, somewhat
415	ついたち	一日	n	for one day, first of month
416	つかう	使う	u-v	to use
417	つかれる	疲れる	ru-v	to get tired, to tire
418	つぎ	次	n	next
419	つく	着く	u-v	to arrive at, to reach
420	つくえ	机	n	desk
421	つくる	作る	u-v	to make, to create
422	つける		ru-v,vt	to turn on (eg a light)
423	つとめる	勤める	ru-v	to serve, to work (for)
424	つまらない		adj	insignificant, boring
425	つめたい	冷たい	adj	cold (to the touch)

#	Kana	Kanji	Type	Definition
426	つよい	強い	adj	strong, powerful
427	て	手	n	hand
428	テープ		n	tape
429	テープレコーダー		n	tape recorder
430	テーブル		n	table
431	でかける	出かける	ru-v	to depart, to go out
432	てがみ	手紙	n	letter
433	できる		ru-v	to be able to
434	でぐち	出口	n	exit
435	テスト		n,vs	test
436	では		expr	with that...
437	デパート		n	department store
438	でも		conj,prt	but, however
439	でる	出る	ru-v	to appear, to leave
440	テレビ		n	television, TV
441	てんき	天気	n	weather
442	でんき	電気	n	electricity, (electric) light
443	でんしゃ	電車	n	electric train
444	でんわ	電話	n,vs	telephone
445	と	戸	n	door (Japanese style)
446	～ど	～度	n-suf	counter for occurrences
447	ドア		n	door (Western style)
448	トイレ		n	toilet
449	どう		adv	how, in what way
450	どうして		adv,int	why?, for what reason

#	Kana	Kanji	Type	Definition
451	どうぞ		adv	please, kindly, by all means
452	どうぶつ	動物	n	animal
453	どうも		adv,int	thanks, very
454	とお	十	num	ten
455	とおい	遠い	adj	far, distant
456	とおか	十日		ten days, tenth day of the month
457	〜とき	〜時	adv,n	at the time of 〜
458	ときどき	時々	adv,n	sometimes
459	とけい	時計	n	watch, clock
460	どこ		n	where, what place
461	ところ	所	n	place
462	とし	年	n	year, age
463	としょかん	図書館	n	library
464	どちら		n	which, which way
465	どっち		n	which one, which way
466	とても		adv	very
467	どなた		n	who
468	となり	隣	n	next to, next door to
469	どの		pren-adj	which
470	とぶ	飛ぶ	u-v	to fly, to hop
471	とまる	止まる	u-v	to come to a halt
472	ともだち	友達	n	friend
473	どようび	土曜日	n-adv,n	Saturday
474	とり	鳥	n	bird
475	とりにく	とり肉	n	chicken meat

#	Kana	Kanji	Type	Definition
476	とる	取る	u-v	to take
477	とる	撮る	u-v	to take (a photo)
478	どれ		n	which (of three or more)
479	どんな			what, what kind of
480	ない		adj	there isn't, doesn't have
481	ナイフ		n	knife
482	なか	中	n	inside, middle, among
483	ながい	長い	adj	long
484	〜ながら		prt	while ~ing, during, although
485	なく	鳴く	u-v	to sing (bird), to make sound (animal)
486	なくす	無くす	u-v	to lose something
487	なぜ		adv	why
488	なつ	夏	n-adv,n-t	summer
489	なつやすみ	夏休み	n	summer vacation, summer holiday
490	〜など		n,n-suf,prt	et cetera
491	ななつ	七つ	n	seven
492	なん/なに	何	int,n	what
493	なのか	七日	n-adv	seven days, seventh day of the month
494	なまえ	名前	n	name
495	ならう	習う	u-v	to learn
496	ならぶ	並ぶ	u-v,vi	to line up, to stand in a line
497	ならべる	並べる	ru-v,vt	to line up, to set up
498	なる		u-v	to become
499	なん〜	何〜		what sort of 〜
500	に	二	num	two

#	Kana	Kanji	Type	Definition
501	にぎやか		na-adj,n	bustling, busy
502	にく	肉	n	meat
503	にし	西	n	west
504	〜にち	〜日		〜 day of the month, for 〜 days
505	にちようび	日曜日	n-adv,n	Sunday
506	にもつ	荷物	n	luggage
507	ニュース		n	news
508	にわ	庭	n	garden
509	〜にん	〜人		counter for people
510	ぬぐ	脱ぐ	u-v	to take off clothes
511	ぬるい	温い	adj	lukewarm
512	ネクタイ		n	tie, necktie
513	ねこ	猫	n	cat
514	ねる	寝る	ru-v	to go to bed, to sleep
515	〜ねん	〜年		〜 years
516	ノート		n	notebook, exercise book
517	のぼる	登る	u-v	to climb
518	のみもの	飲み物	n	drink, beverage
519	のむ	飲む	u-v	to drink
520	のる	乗る	u-v	to get on, to ride in, to board
521	は	歯	n	tooth
522	パーティー		n	party
523	はい		conj,int	yes
524	〜はい	〜杯	n	counter for cupfuls
525	はいざら	灰皿	n	ashtray

#	Kana	Kanji	Type	Definition
526	はいる	入る	u-v	to enter, to contain, to hold
527	はがき	葉書	n	postcard
528	はく		u-v	to wear, to put on (trousers)
529	はこ	箱	n	box
530	はし	橋	n	bridge
531	はし		n	chopsticks
532	はじまる	始まる	u-v,vi	to begin
533	はじめ	初め/始め	expr	beginning, start
534	はじめて	初めて	adv,n	for the first time
535	はしる	走る	u-v	to run
536	バス		n	bus
537	バター		n	butter
538	はたち	二十歳	n	20 years old, 20th year
539	はたらく	働く	u-v	to work
540	はち	八	num	eight
541	はつか	二十日	n	twenty days, 20th day of the month
542	はな	花	n	flower
543	はな	鼻	n	nose
544	はなし	話	n	talk, story
545	はなす	話す	u-v	to speak
546	はは	母	n	(one's own) mother
547	はやい	早い	adj	early
548	はやい	速い	adj	quick, fast
549	はる	春	n-adv,n-t	spring
550	はる	貼る	u-v	to stick, to paste

#	Kana	Kanji	Type	Definition
551	はれ	晴れ	ru-v	clear weather
552	はれる	晴れる	ru-v	to be sunny
553	はん	半	n-adv,n,n-suf	half
554	ばん	晩	n-adv,n-t	evening
555	～ばん	～番	n-adv,n-t	～st/th best
556	パン		n	bread
557	ハンカチ		n	handkerchief
558	ばんごう	番号	n	number
559	ばんごはん	晩御飯	n	dinner, evening meal
560	はんぶん	半分		half
561	ひがし	東	n	east
562	～ひき	～匹		counter for small animals
563	ひく	引く	u-v	to pull
564	ひく	弾く	u-v	to play (piano, guitar)
565	ひくい	低い	adj	short, low
566	ひこうき	飛行機	n	aeroplane, airplane
567	ひだり	左	n	left hand side
568	ひと	人	n	man, person
569	ひとつ	一つ	n	one
570	ひとつき	一月	n	one month
571	ひとり	一人	n	one person
572	ひま	暇	na-adj,n	free time, leisure
573	ひゃく	百	num	100, hundred
574	びょういん	病院	n	hospital
575	びょうき	病気	n	illness, disease, sickness

#	Kana	Kanji	Type	Definition
576	ひらがな	平仮名	n	hiragana
577	ひる	昼	n-adv,n-t	noon, daytime
578	ひるごはん	昼御飯	n	lunch, midday meal
579	ひろい	広い	adj	spacious, wide
580	フィルム		n	film (roll of)
581	ふうとう	封筒	n	envelope
582	プール		n	swimming pool
583	フォーク		n	fork
584	ふく	吹く	u-v	to blow (wind, etc)
585	ふく	服	n,n-suf	clothes
586	ふたつ	二つ	n	two
587	ぶたにく	豚肉	n	pork
588	ふたり	二人	n	two people
589	ふつか	二日	n	second day of the month, two days
590	ふとい	太い	adj	fat, thick
591	ふゆ	冬	n-adv,n-t	winter
592	ふる	降る	u-v	to precipitate, to fall (e.g. rain)
593	ふるい	古い	adj	old (not person), aged, ancient
594	ふろ		n	bath
595	～ふん	～分	suf	～minutes
596	ぶんしょう	文章	suf	sentence, text
597	ページ		n	page
598	へた	下手	na-adj,n	unskillful, poor
599	ベッド		n	bed
600	ペット		n	pet

#	Kana	Kanji	Type	Definition
601	へや	部屋	n	room
602	へん	辺	n	area, vicinity
603	ペン		n	pen
604	べんきょう（する）	勉強	n,vs	study, diligence
605	べんり	便利	na-adj,n	convenient, handy
606	ほう			way
607	ぼうし	帽子	n	hat
608	ボールペン		n	ball-point pen
609	ほか	外	n	other place, the rest
610	ポケット		n	pocket
611	ほしい	欲しい	adj	want, in need of, desire
612	ポスト		n	post
613	ほそい	細い	adj	thin, slender, fine
614	ボタン		n	button
615	ホテル		n	hotel
616	ほん	本	n	book
617	〜ほん	〜本		counter for long cylindrical things
618	ほんだな	本棚	n	bookshelves
619	ほんとう		adv	reality, truth
620	〜まい	〜枚		counter for flat things
621	まいあさ	毎朝	n-adv,n-t	every morning
622	まいげつ/まいつき	毎月	n-adv,n	every month, monthly
623	まいしゅう	毎週	n-adv,n-t	every week
624	まいにち	毎日	n-adv,n-t	every day
625	まいねん/まいとし	毎年	n-t	every year, annually

#	Kana	Kanji	Type	Definition
626	まいばん	毎晩	n-adv,n-t	every night
627	まえ	前	n-adv,n-t,suf	before, in front
628	～まえ	～前	suf	in front of ～
629	まがる	曲る	u-v	to turn, to bend
630	まずい		adj	unappetising, unpleasant (taste)
631	また		adv,conj,n	again, and
632	まだ		adv	yet, still, besides
633	まち	町	n	town, city
634	まつ	待つ	u-v	to wait
635	まっすぐ		na-adj,adv,n	straight (ahead), direct
636	マッチ		n	match
637	まど	窓	n	window
638	まるい	丸い/円い	adj	round, circular
639	まん	万	adv,num	ten thousand, everything
640	まんねんひつ	万年筆	n	fountain pen
641	みがく	磨く	u-v	to brush (teeth)
642	みぎ	右	n	right hand side
643	みじかい	短い	adj	short
644	みず	水	n	water
645	みせ	店	n,n-suf	store, shop, establishment
646	みせる	見せる	ru-v	to show, to display
647	みち	道	n	road, street
648	みっか	三日	n	three days, third day of the month
649	みっつ	三つ	n	three
650	みどり	緑	n	green

#	Kana	Kanji	Type	Definition
651	みなさん	皆さん	n	everyone
652	みなみ	南	n,vs	South, proceeding south
653	みみ	耳	n	ear
654	みる	見る	ru-v	to see, to watch
655	みんな		adv,n	all, everyone, everybody
656	むいか	六日		six days, sixth (day of month)
657	むこう	向こう	n	beyond, over there
658	むずかしい	難しい	adj	difficult
659	むっつ	六つ	num	six
660	むら	村	num	village
661	め	目	n	eye, eyeball
662	メートル		n	metre, meter
663	めがね	眼鏡	n	spectacles, glasses
664	もう		adv,int	already
665	もう		adv,int	again
666	もくようび	木曜日	n-adv,n	Thursday
667	もしもし		conj,int	hello (on phone)
668	もつ	持つ	u-v	(1) to hold, to carry, (2) to possess
669	もっと		adv	more, longer, farther
670	もの	物	n	thing, object
671	もん	門	n,n-suf	gate
672	もんだい	問題	n	problem, question
673	～や	屋	n	～ shop
674	やおや	八百屋	n	greengrocer
675	やさい	野菜	n	vegetable

#	Kana	Kanji	Type	Definition
676	やさしい	易しい	adj	easy, plain, simple
677	やすい	安い	adj	cheap, inexpensive
678	やすみ	休み	n	rest, vacation, holiday
679	やすむ	休む	u-v,vi	to rest, to have a break, to take a day off
680	やっつ	八つ	num	eight
681	やま	山	n	mountain
682	やる		u-v	to do
683	ゆうがた	夕方	n-adv,n-t	evening
684	ゆうはん	夕飯	n	dinner
685	ゆうびんきょく	郵便局	n	post office
686	ゆうべ	昨夜	n	last night
687	ゆうめい	有名	na-adj,n	famous
688	ゆき	雪	n	snow
689	ゆっくり・と		adv,n	slowly, at ease
690	ようか	八日	n	eight days, the eighth (day of the month)
691	ようふく	洋服	n	Western-style clothes
692	よく		adv	frequently, often
693	よく		adv	well, skillfully
694	よこ	横	n	beside, side, width
695	よっか	四日	n	(1) 4th day of month, (2) four days
696	よっつ	四つ	n	four
697	よぶ	呼ぶ	u-v	to call out, to invite
698	よむ	読む	u-v	to read
699	よる	夜	n	evening, night
700	よわい	弱い	adj	weak, feable

#	Kana	Kanji	Type	Definition
701	らいげつ	来月	n-adv,n-t	next month
702	らいしゅう	来週		next week
703	らいねん	来年	n-adv,n-t	next year
704	ラジオ		n	radio
705	ラジカセ		n	radio cassette player
706	りっぱ		na-adj,n	splendid, fine
707	りゅうがくせい	留学生	n	overseas student
708	りょうしん	両親	n	parents, both parents
709	りょうり	料理	n,vs	cooking, cuisine
710	りょこう	旅行	n,vs	travel, trip
711	れい	零	n	zero, nought
712	れいぞうこ	冷蔵庫	n	refrigerator
713	レコード		n	record
714	レストラン		n	restaurant
715	れんしゅう(する)	練習	n,vs	(to) practice
716	ろうか	廊下	n	corridor
717	ろく	六	num	six
718	ワイシャツ		n	shirt (lit: white shirt), business shirt
719	わかい	若い	adj	young
720	わかる	分かる	u-v	to understand
721	わすれる	忘れる	ru-v	to forget
722	わたし	私	adj-no,n	I, myself
723	わたくし	私	adj-no,n	I, myself
724	わたす	渡す	u-v	to pass over, to hand over
725	わたる	渡る	u-v	to cross over, to go across
726	わるい	悪い	adj	bad, inferior

ざ

じ

ず

ぜ

ぞ

だ

ぢ

づ

で

ど

da

だいがく　　　 university
だいじょうぶ　 all right
だいどころ　　 kitchen

za

ざっし　　　　 Magazine

dzi

ji

じどうしゃ　　 Automobile
じしょ　　　　 Dictionary
じてんしゃ　　 Bicycle

dzu

zu

ズボン　　　　 Trousers

de

でんしゃ　　　 electric train
でんわ　　　　 telephone

ze

ぜんぶ　　　　 All

do

どうして　　　 for what reason
どうぶつ　　　 animal
どうも　　　　 thanks

zo

ば

び

ぶ

べ

ぼ

ぱ

ぴ

ぷ

ぺ

ぽ

pa

パーティー party

pi

pu

pe

ページ page
ペット pet
ペン pen

po

ポケット pocket
ポスト post

ba

ばんごう number
ばんごはん evening meal

bi

びょういん hospital
びょうき illness

bu

ぶたにく pork
ぶんしょう sentence,text

be

べんきょうする to study
べんり useful,
convenient

bo

ぼうし hat

きゃ	みゃ
しゃ	りゃ
ちゃ	きゅ
にゃ	しゅ
ひゃ	ちゅ

mya

kya

rya

sha
しゃしん　　　photograph

kyu
ぎゅうにく　　Beef
ぎゅうにゅう　Milk

cha
ちゃいろ　　　brown
ちゃわん　　　rice bowl

shu
しゅくだい　　homework

nya

chu

hya
ひゃく　　　hundred

にゅ　　しょ

ひゅ　　ちょ

みゅ　　にょ

りゅ　　ひょ

きょ　　みょ

sho

しょうゆ   soy sauce
しょくどう   dining hall

cho

ちょうど   exactly
ちょっと   somewhat

nyo

hyo

myo

nyu

hyu

myu

ryu

kyo

きょう   Today
きょうしつ   Classroom
きょうだい （humble）siblings

Hiragana flash cards

りょ
ん

ryo

n

Hiragana flash cards

ア カ

イ キ

ウ ク

エ ケ

オ コ

ka

かぜ	a cold
かぞく	Family
カップ	Cup

a

あたたかい	warm
あたま	head
あつい	hot

ki

きたない	Dirty
きって	postage stamp
きっぷ	Ticket

i

いけ	pond
いしゃ	medical doctor
いす	chair

ku

くるま	car, vehicle
くろい	black
クラス	Class

u

うる	to sell
うるさい	noisy, annoying
うわぎ	jacket

ke

| けさ | this morning |
| けす | to erase, to turn off |

e

えき	station
エレベーター	elevator
えんぴつ	pencil

ko

コピーする	to copy
コーヒー	Coffee
コート	coat, tennis court

o

おちゃ	green tea
おてあらい	bathroom
おんがく	Music

Katakana flash cards

タ

チ

ツ

テ

ト

サ

シ

ス

セ

ソ

ta

たいしかん	embassy
たかい	tall, expensive
タクシー	taxi

chi

| ちず | map |
| ちかてつ | underground train |

tsu

つくる	to make
つける	to turn on
つよい	powerful

te

テープ	tape
テーブル	table
テレビ	television

to

トイレ	toilet
とおい	far
とけい	watch, clock

sa

さいふ	Wallet
さかな	Fish
さくぶん	composition

shi

しかし	However
しずか	Quiet
しつもん	Question

su

スカート	Skirt
ストーブ	Heater
スプーン	Spoon

se

セーター	sweater, jumper
せびろ	business suit
せんたく	Washing

so

そと	Outside
そば	near, beside
それから	after that

Katakana flash cards

ハ ヒ フ ヘ ホ

ナ ニ ヌ ネ ノ

ha

はいる   to enter,
             to contain
ハンカチ   handkerchief

hi

ひく   to pull
ひこうき   aeroplane
ひろい   spacious,wide

fu

フィルム   roll of film
フォーク   fork
ふく   to blow

he

へや   room
へた   unskillful
へん   area

ho

ホテル   hotel
ほんだな   bookshelves
ほそい   thin

na

など   et cetera
ナイフ   knife

ni

ニュース   news
にし   west
にちようび   Sunday

nu

ぬるい   luke warm
ぬぐ   to take off
            clothes

ne

ネクタイ   tie, necktie
ねる   to go to bed,
            to sleep

no

ノート   notebook
のぼる   to climb
のみもの   a drink

Katakana flash cards

マ	ヤ
ミ	ユ
ム	ヨ
メ	ワ
モ	ヲ

ya

やすみ	rest, holiday
やすむ	to rest
やま	mountain

ma

マッチ	match
マッチ	match
まるい	round, circular

yu

ゆく	to go
ゆうべ	last night
ゆうはん	dinner

mi

みせ	shop
みせる	to show
みなみ	south

yo

よわい	weak
よる	evening, night
よっつ	four

mu

むっつ	six
むこう	over there
むいか	six days

wa

ワイシャツ	business shirt
わかい	young

me

メートル	metre

o

mo

もういちど	again
もっと	more
もの	thing

Katakana flash cards

ラ リ ル レ ロ

ガ ギ グ ゲ ゴ

ga

がいこくじん	Foreigner
がくせい	Student
がっこう	School

ra

| ラジオ | radio |

ラジカセ / ラジオカセット

radio cassette player

gi

| ぎんこう | Bank |

ri

りょうしん both parents
りょうり cuisine
りょこう travel

gu

| グラム | Gram |

ru

ge

げつようび	Monday
げんかん	entry hall
げんき	health, vitality

re

| レコード | record |
| レストラン | restaurant |

go

ごご	Five
	afternoon
ごぜん	morning

ro

| ろうか | corridor |
| ろく | six |

Katakana flash cards

ザ
ジ
ズ
ゼ
ゾ

da
だいがく   university
だいじょうぶ   all right
だいどころ   kitchen

za
ざっし   Magazine

dzi

ji
じどうしゃ   Automobile
じしょ   Dictionary
じてんしゃ   Bicycle

dzu
ズボン   Trousers

zu
ズボン   Trousers

de
デパート   department store

ze
ゼロ   Zero

do
ドア   Western style door

zo

バ

ビ

ブ

ベ

ボ

パ

ピ

プ

ペ

ポ

pa

パーティー   party
パン   bread

ba

バター   butter

pi

bi

びょういん   hospital
びょうき   illness

pu

プール   swimming pool

bu

ぶたにく   pork
ぶんしょう   sentence,text

pe

ページ   page
ペット   pet
ペン   pen

be

べんきょうする   to study
べんり   useful, convenient

po

ポケット   pocket
ポスト   post

bo

ボールペン   ball-point pen
ボタン   button

キャ	ミャ
シャ	リャ
チャ	キュ
ニャ	シュ
ヒャ	チュ

mya

rya

kyu
ぎゅうにく Beef
ぎゅうにゅう　　Milk

shu
しゅくだい　　homework

chu

kya

sha
シャツ　　　　Shirt
シャワー　　　Shower

cha
ちゃいろ　　　brown
ちゃわん　　　rice bowl

nya

hya
ひゃく　　　　hundred

ニュ	シ ョ
ヒュ	チ ョ
ミュ	ニ ョ
リュ	ヒ ョ
キ ョ	ミ ョ

sho

しょうゆ   soy sauce
しょくどう   dining hall

nyu

cho

ちょうど   exactly
ちょっと   somewhat

hyu

nyo

myu

hyo

ryu

myo

kyo

きょう   Today
きょうしつ   Classroom
きょうだい   (humble) siblings

    Katakana flash cards

リョ
ン

ryo

n

Flash cards

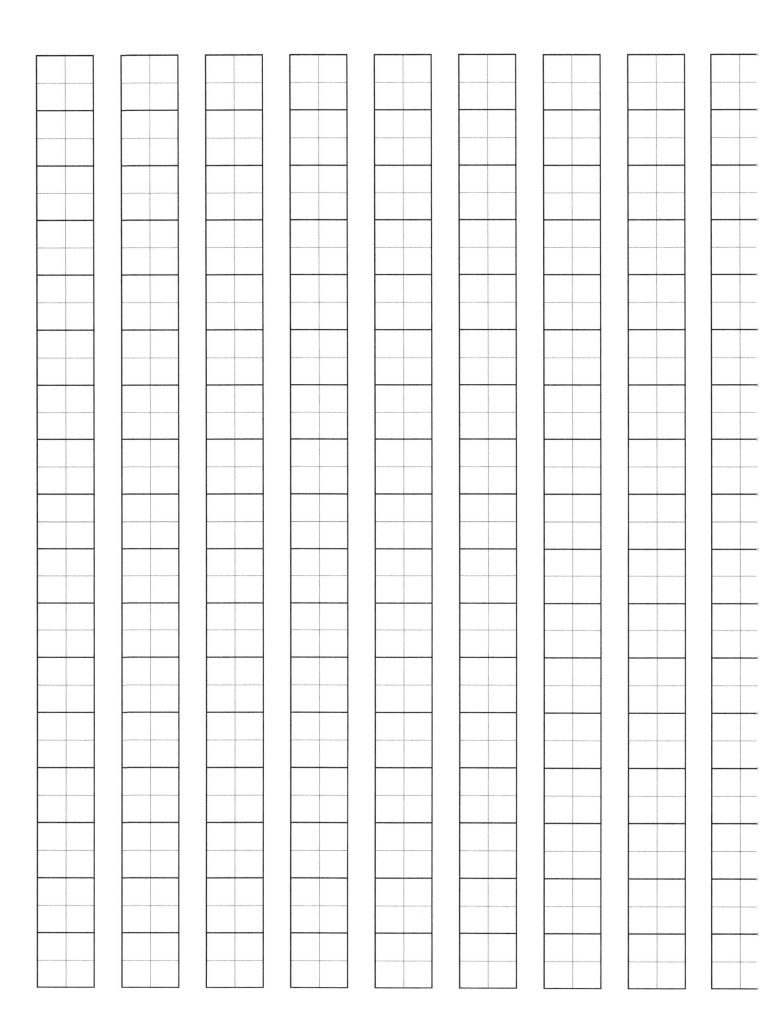

Made in the USA
Las Vegas, NV
26 September 2021